ALIGNING
—— YOUR ——
INNER SELF
Self Meditation Journal

By Christin

All R

D1445652

Art Design by Jordan Douglas *Goldin Productions*
Edited by Miles M. Spann

Disclaimer:
No part of this publication may be reproduced, distributed, or transmitted in any form or by any
means, including photocopying, recording, or other electronic methods, without prior written per-
mission of the author.

Introduction

Over the years I struggled with low self-esteem, negative thinking, anxiety, depression, lack of self-worth and many other things. I fought battles within myself every day and often felt lost. Battles in which no one even knew I was fighting. Battles, I was too ashamed to even share with anyone. I didn't trust people with my deepest darkest fears because I thought they would judge me. So, I tried to bottle it in. My struggle with suppression is that I couldn't contain it. I had no other option but to search within myself for the root of all these feelings. I turned to writing as an outlet.

I wrote in order to give all the thoughts running through my head a space to live outside of me. Having these words on paper, helped me dissect and organize my thoughts and feelings. The more I wrote, the more awareness I gained of myself. I realized that I was struggling with my identity. My Body, Soul and Spirit were out of alignment. My mission is to share with you the tools and techniques to align your inner self.

ALIGNING YOUR INNER SELF

I hope this meditation journal serves as a light unto your path as you journey to discover your true inner self, by aligning your Body, Soul, and Spirit.

Self-Care is the act of practicing the ability to be aware of mental, emotional and physical health needs.

Examples are eating daily, showering, getting enough sleep, exercising daily, etc.

We often tend to our physical needs and neglect our emotional/mental needs.

Self-Compassion is having patience, understanding, and unconditional love towards yourself.

It is by practicing self-compassion that we begin to align our body, spirit, and soul.

Date: /   /   Time   :   am – pm   Location: _____

Today I feel_____ because _____

_____

_____

What are you grateful for today?

I am grateful for _____

I am grateful for _____

I am grateful for _____

Daily Goals

Emotional

    I will intentionally work on _____

    How will you work on this goal? _____

Thoughts

    I will intentionally work on _____

    How will you work on this goal? _____

Body

    I will intentionally work on _____

    How will you work on this goal? _____

I am a STRONG person because_____

I LOVE that I am_____

Today, I will practice self-compassion by: _____

_____

_____

_____

What words would you use to describe your personality?

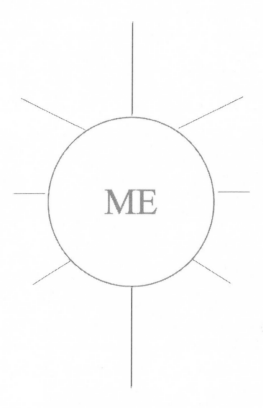

Date: /   /   Time   :   am – pm   Location: _____

Today I feel_____ because _____
_____
_____

What are you grateful for today?

I am grateful for _____

I am grateful for _____

I am grateful for _____

Daily Goals

Emotional
    I will intentionally work on _____
    How will you work on this goal? _____

Thoughts
    I will intentionally work on _____
    How will you work on this goal? _____

Body
    I will intentionally work on _____
    How will you work on this goal? _____

I am a STRONG person because_____
I LOVE that I am_____

Today, I will practice self-compassion by: _____
_____
_____
_____

What makes you unique?

*I am unique because...*_____

*I am unique because...*_____

*I am unique because...*_____

*I am unique because...*_____

*I am unique because...*_____

*I am unique because...*_____

*I am unique because...*_____

*I am unique because...*_____

*I am unique because...*_____

*I am unique because...*_____

Date: /   /   Time :   am – pm   Location: _____

Today I feel_____ because _____
_____
_____

What are you grateful for today?

I am grateful for _____

I am grateful for _____

I am grateful for _____

                         Daily Goals

Emotional
    I will intentionally work on _____
    How will you work on this goal? _____

Thoughts
    I will intentionally work on _____
    How will you work on this goal? _____

Body
    I will intentionally work on _____
    How will you work on this goal? _____

I am a STRONG person because_____
I LOVE that I am_____

Today, I will practice self-compassion by: _____
_____
_____
_____

What are 5 things that you value?

1.)

2.)

3.)

4.)

5.)

Date: /   /   Time   :   am – pm   Location: _____

Today I feel_____ because _____
_____
_____

What are you grateful for today?

I am grateful for _____

I am grateful for _____

I am grateful for _____

                        Daily Goals
Emotional
        I will intentionally work on _____
        How will you work on this goal? _____

Thoughts
        I will intentionally work on _____
        How will you work on this goal? _____

Body
        I will intentionally work on _____
        How will you work on this goal? _____

I am a STRONG person because_____
I LOVE that I am_____

Today, I will practice self-compassion by: _____
_____
_____
_____

Write a poem that describes what unconditional love means to you.

Incorporate your 5 senses: Sight (vision), Hearing (audition), Taste (gustation), Smell (olfaction), and Touch (somatosensation)

Date: /   /   Time   :   am – pm   Location: _____

Today I feel_____ because _____

_____

_____

What are you grateful for today?

I am grateful for _____

I am grateful for _____

I am grateful for _____

Daily Goals

Emotional

    I will intentionally work on _____

    How will you work on this goal? _____

Thoughts

    I will intentionally work on _____

    How will you work on this goal? _____

Body

    I will intentionally work on _____

    How will you work on this goal? _____

I am a STRONG person because_____

I LOVE that I am_____

Today, I will practice self-compassion by: _____

_____

_____

_____

Make a drawing about a friendship that is important to you.
(Don't worry about it being a "good" drawing.)

Reflection for the day: Are you a good friend to others?

Date: / /   Time   :   am – pm   Location: _____

Today I feel_____ because _____

_____

_____

What are you grateful for today?

I am grateful for _____

I am grateful for _____

I am grateful for _____

Daily Goals

Emotional
  I will intentionally work on _____
  How will you work on this goal? _____

Thoughts
  I will intentionally work on _____
  How will you work on this goal? _____

Body
  I will intentionally work on _____
  How will you work on this goal? _____

I am a STRONG person because_____
I LOVE that I am_____

Today, I will practice self-compassion by: _____

_____

_____

_____

Write a thank you letter to someone that has been supportive to you.

*Dear*_____,

Thank you.

Date: / /   Time :   am – pm   Location: _____

Today I feel_____ because _____
_____
_____

What are you grateful for today?

I am grateful for _____

I am grateful for _____

I am grateful for _____

Daily Goals

Emotional

    I will intentionally work on _____

    How will you work on this goal? _____

Thoughts

    I will intentionally work on _____

    How will you work on this goal? _____

Body

    I will intentionally work on _____

    How will you work on this goal? _____

I am a STRONG person because_____

I LOVE that I am_____

Today, I will practice self-compassion by: _____
_____
_____
_____

When you experience happiness, where do you feel it in your body? (heart, chest, stomach, etc.)

For example: I smile really big and get a burst of energy in my arms and legs.

Refelction of the day: What song do you play that instantly takes you to a place of happiness?

Date: / /   Time :   am – pm   Location: _____

Today I feel_____ because _____

_____

_____

What are you grateful for today?

I am grateful for _____

I am grateful for _____

I am grateful for _____

                        Daily Goals
Emotional
        I will intentionally work on _____
        How will you work on this goal? _____

Thoughts
        I will intentionally work on _____
        How will you work on this goal? _____

Body
        I will intentionally work on _____
        How will you work on this goal? _____

I am a STRONG person because_____
I LOVE that I am_____

Today, I will practice self-compassion by: _____

_____

_____

_____

Where do you go to clear your head? (Park, Beach, Church, etc.)
Why?

Reflection of the day: Is there a specific place where you feel the most connected to the universe?

Date: / /   Time   :   am – pm   Location: _____

Today I feel_____ because _____

_____

_____

What are you grateful for today?

I am grateful for _____

I am grateful for _____

I am grateful for _____

                           Daily Goals
Emotional
        I will intentionally work on _____
        How will you work on this goal? _____

Thoughts
        I will intentionally work on _____
        How will you work on this goal? _____

Body
        I will intentionally work on _____
        How will you work on this goal? _____

I am a STRONG person because_____
I LOVE that I am_____

Today, I will practice self-compassion by: _____

_____

_____

_____

Write a poem to your higher power.

Reflection of the day: What do you think you need to do to strengthen your connection to your higher power?

Date: /   /   Time   :   am – pm   Location: _____

Today I feel_____ because _____

_____

_____

What are you grateful for today?

I am grateful for _____

I am grateful for _____

I am grateful for _____

                        Daily Goals
Emotional
        I will intentionally work on _____
        How will you work on this goal? _____

Thoughts
        I will intentionally work on _____
        How will you work on this goal? _____

Body
        I will intentionally work on _____
        How will you work on this goal? _____

I am a STRONG person because_____
I LOVE that I am_____

Today, I will practice self-compassion by: _____

_____

_____

_____

Go out and do something kind for a stranger.

Journal what you did, how they reacted, and how it made you feel.

Date: /   /   Time   :   am – pm   Location: _____

Today I feel_____ because _____
_____
_____

What are you grateful for today?

I am grateful for _____

I am grateful for _____

I am grateful for _____

Daily Goals
Emotional
  I will intentionally work on _____
  How will you work on this goal? _____

Thoughts
  I will intentionally work on _____
  How will you work on this goal? _____

Body
  I will intentionally work on _____
  How will you work on this goal? _____

I am a STRONG person because_____
I LOVE that I am_____

Today, I will practice self-compassion by: _____
_____
_____
_____

Write a short story about a good community experience you had.
(This can be family, friends, school, work, etc.)

Date: /   /   Time   :   am – pm   Location: _____

Today I feel_____ because _____
_____
_____

What are you grateful for today?

I am grateful for _____

I am grateful for _____

I am grateful for _____

                              Daily Goals
Emotional
        I will intentionally work on _____
        How will you work on this goal? _____

Thoughts
        I will intentionally work on _____
        How will you work on this goal? _____

Body
        I will intentionally work on _____
        How will you work on this goal? _____

I am a STRONG person because_____
I LOVE that I am_____

Today, I will practice self-compassion by: _____
_____
_____
_____

Draw an image of your family.

Date: /   /   Time   :   am – pm   Location: _____

Today I feel_____ because _____
_____
_____

What are you grateful for today?

I am grateful for _____

I am grateful for _____

I am grateful for _____

                        Daily Goals
Emotional
        I will intentionally work on _____
        How will you work on this goal? _____

Thoughts
        I will intentionally work on _____
        How will you work on this goal? _____

Body
        I will intentionally work on _____
        How will you work on this goal? _____

I am a STRONG person because_____
I LOVE that I am_____

Today, I will practice self-compassion by: _____
_____
_____
_____

What are you self-conscious about and why?

Tell someone you trust about your insecurity and be completely honest.

Date: /   /   Time   :   am – pm   Location: _____

Today I feel_____ because _____

_____

_____

What are you grateful for today?

I am grateful for _____

I am grateful for _____

I am grateful for _____

Daily Goals

Emotional

    I will intentionally work on _____

    How will you work on this goal? _____

Thoughts

    I will intentionally work on _____

    How will you work on this goal? _____

Body

    I will intentionally work on _____

    How will you work on this goal? _____

I am a STRONG person because_____

I LOVE that I am_____

Today, I will practice self-compassion by: _____

_____

_____

_____

Draw an outline of your body. Which part do you struggle to love and why?

Reflection of the day: What can you do to accept that part of your body?

Date: /   /   Time   :   am – pm   Location: _____

Today I feel_____ because _____
_____
_____

What are you grateful for today?

I am grateful for _____

I am grateful for _____

I am grateful for _____

                        Daily Goals
Emotional
        I will intentionally work on _____
        How will you work on this goal? _____

Thoughts
        I will intentionally work on _____
        How will you work on this goal? _____

Body
        I will intentionally work on _____
        How will you work on this goal? _____

I am a STRONG person because_____
I LOVE that I am_____

Today, I will practice self-compassion by: _____
_____
_____
_____

The most disappointed I've ever been was when...

Have you let this go? *If not, write three ways that you can.*

-

-

-

Date: / /   Time   :   am – pm   Location: _____

Today I feel_____ because _____
_____
_____

What are you grateful for today?

I am grateful for _____

I am grateful for _____

I am grateful for _____

Daily Goals

Emotional
    I will intentionally work on _____
    How will you work on this goal? _____

Thoughts
    I will intentionally work on _____
    How will you work on this goal? _____

Body
    I will intentionally work on _____
    How will you work on this goal? _____

I am a STRONG person because_____
I LOVE that I am_____

Today, I will practice self-compassion by: _____
_____
_____
_____

Write a confession.

Nobody knows that I...

Now go to a mirror and read it out loud to yourself.

Journal how it felt to write it versus saying it aloud.

Date:　/　/　　　　　　　　　Time　:　　am – pm　　　　Location: _____

Today I feel_____ because _____
_____
_____

What are you grateful for today?

I am grateful for _____

I am grateful for _____

I am grateful for _____

                       Daily Goals

Emotional
      I will intentionally work on _____
      How will you work on this goal? _____

Thoughts
      I will intentionally work on _____
      How will you work on this goal? _____

Body
      I will intentionally work on _____
      How will you work on this goal? _____

I am a STRONG person because_____
I LOVE that I am_____

Today, I will practice self-compassion by: _____
_____
_____
_____

Is there someone in your life that you need to forgive?
Write a letter of forgiveness to them. (You can also write a letter to yourself)

Date: / /   Time :   am – pm   Location: _____

Today I feel_____ because _____
_____
_____

What are you grateful for today?

I am grateful for _____

I am grateful for _____

I am grateful for _____

Daily Goals

Emotional
    I will intentionally work on _____
    How will you work on this goal? _____

Thoughts
    I will intentionally work on _____
    How will you work on this goal? _____

Body
    I will intentionally work on _____
    How will you work on this goal? _____

I am a STRONG person because_____
I LOVE that I am_____

Today, I will practice self-compassion by: _____
_____
_____
_____

What color do you associate anger with?
Make a doodle of what anger feels like in your body.

Relfection of the day: How do you process anger?

Date: /   /   Time   :   am – pm   Location: _____

Today I feel_____ because _____
_____
_____

What are you grateful for today?

I am grateful for _____

I am grateful for _____

I am grateful for _____

                              Daily Goals
Emotional
        I will intentionally work on _____
        How will you work on this goal? _____

Thoughts
        I will intentionally work on _____
        How will you work on this goal? _____

Body
        I will intentionally work on _____
        How will you work on this goal? _____

I am a STRONG person because_____
I LOVE that I am_____

Today, I will practice self-compassion by: _____
_____
_____
_____

The next time you become upset try this:

- *Count to five*

- *Take three deep breaths*
  (in through your nose and out through your mouth)

- *Push your toes and heels into the ground to transfer*
  this emotion into your feet

- *Verbalize to the person what they just*
  said or did to make you upset

- *Be conscious of your tone, choice of words,*
  and facial expressions

- *Come to a solution as to how you can move forward*
  from this experience

- *Let it go*

Date: / /   Time   :   am – pm   Location: _____

Today I feel_____ because _____
_____
_____

What are you grateful for today?

I am grateful for _____

I am grateful for _____

I am grateful for _____

Daily Goals
Emotional
    I will intentionally work on _____
    How will you work on this goal? _____

Thoughts
    I will intentionally work on _____
    How will you work on this goal? _____

Body
    I will intentionally work on _____
    How will you work on this goal? _____

I am a STRONG person because_____
I LOVE that I am_____

Today, I will practice self-compassion by: _____
_____
_____
_____

If you could go back in time and change one thing from your past, what would it be?

Reflection of the day: If you could go forward in time and know one thing from your future, what would you want to know?

ALIGNING YOUR INNER SELF

40

Date: /   /   Time   :   am – pm   Location: _____

Today I feel_____ because _____

_____

_____

What are you grateful for today?

I am grateful for _____

I am grateful for _____

I am grateful for _____

                        Daily Goals
Emotional
        I will intentionally work on _____
        How will you work on this goal? _____

Thoughts
        I will intentionally work on _____
        How will you work on this goal? _____

Body
        I will intentionally work on _____
        How will you work on this goal? _____

I am a STRONG person because_____
I LOVE that I am_____

Today, I will practice self-compassion by: _____

_____

_____

_____

Yes / No

Write a list *of things you wish you said* **Yes** *to:*

Write a list *of things you wish you said* **No** *to:*

Date: /   /   Time   :   am – pm   Location: _____

Today I feel_____ because _____
_____
_____

What are you grateful for today?

I am grateful for _____

I am grateful for _____

I am grateful for _____

                        Daily Goals
Emotional
        I will intentionally work on _____
        How will you work on this goal? _____

Thoughts
        I will intentionally work on _____
        How will you work on this goal? _____

Body
        I will intentionally work on _____
        How will you work on this goal? _____

I am a STRONG person because_____
I LOVE that I am_____

Today, I will practice self-compassion by: _____
_____
_____
_____

What are three things you would do if you had infinite resources?

1.)

2.)

3.)

Date: /   /   Time   :   am – pm   Location: _____

Today I feel_____ because _____
_____
_____

What are you grateful for today?

I am grateful for _____

I am grateful for _____

I am grateful for _____

                          Daily Goals
Emotional
        I will intentionally work on _____
        How will you work on this goal? _____

Thoughts
        I will intentionally work on _____
        How will you work on this goal? _____

Body
        I will intentionally work on _____
        How will you work on this goal? _____

I am a STRONG person because_____
I LOVE that I am_____

Today, I will practice self-compassion by: _____
_____
_____
_____

Write about a time that you felt truly proud of something good you did.

What are your strengths?

-

-

-

-

-

What are your weakness'?

-

-

-

-

-

Date: /   /   Time   :   am – pm   Location: _____

Today I feel_____ because _____
_____
_____

What are you grateful for today?

I am grateful for _____

I am grateful for _____

I am grateful for _____

                    Daily Goals
Emotional
        I will intentionally work on _____
        How will you work on this goal? _____

Thoughts
        I will intentionally work on _____
        How will you work on this goal? _____

Body
        I will intentionally work on _____
        How will you work on this goal? _____

I am a STRONG person because_____
I LOVE that I am_____

Today, I will practice self-compassion by: _____
_____
_____
_____

What are your short-term/long-term goals?

Short-Term:

1.)

2.)

3.)

Long-Term:

1.)

2.)

3.)

Reflection of the day: What can you do this week to push you closer to your goals?

Date: /   /   Time   :   am – pm   Location: _____

Today I feel_____ because _____

_____

_____

What are you grateful for today?

I am grateful for _____

I am grateful for _____

I am grateful for _____

                        Daily Goals
Emotional
        I will intentionally work on _____
        How will you work on this goal? _____

Thoughts
        I will intentionally work on _____
        How will you work on this goal? _____

Body
        I will intentionally work on _____
        How will you work on this goal? _____

I am a STRONG person because_____
I LOVE that I am_____

Today, I will practice self-compassion by: _____

_____

_____

_____

Make a vision board.

Find a magazine and cut out images and words that relate to your goals.

Date: /   /   Time   :   am – pm   Location: _____

Today I feel_____ because _____

_____

_____

What are you grateful for today?

I am grateful for _____

I am grateful for _____

I am grateful for _____

                         Daily Goals

Emotional

    I will intentionally work on _____

    How will you work on this goal? _____

Thoughts

    I will intentionally work on _____

    How will you work on this goal? _____

Body

    I will intentionally work on _____

    How will you work on this goal? _____

I am a STRONG person because_____

I LOVE that I am_____

Today, I will practice self-compassion by: _____

_____

_____

_____

Why do you think having a routine is important?

What would you like your morning routine to be?
Example: Wake up at 7:30am, make coffee, go for a run.

What would you like your nightly routine to be?
Example: Cook dinner, check emails, take a shower before bed.

Date: /   /   Time   :   am – pm   Location: _____

Today I feel_____ because _____

_____

_____

What are you grateful for today?

I am grateful for _____

I am grateful for _____

I am grateful for _____

Daily Goals

Emotional

    I will intentionally work on _____

    How will you work on this goal? _____

Thoughts

    I will intentionally work on _____

    How will you work on this goal? _____

Body

    I will intentionally work on _____

    How will you work on this goal? _____

I am a STRONG person because_____

I LOVE that I am_____

Today, I will practice self-compassion by: _____

_____

_____

_____

Write a To-Do List for today.
Prioritize what needs to get done first.

Highlight or Check off task when completed.

1.)

2.)

3.)

Reflection of the day: Try to make this a daily habit and see how it changes your productivity every day.

Date: / /   Time   :   am – pm   Location: _____

Today I feel_____ because _____
_____
_____

What are you grateful for today?

I am grateful for _____

I am grateful for _____

I am grateful for _____

                        Daily Goals
Emotional
        I will intentionally work on _____
        How will you work on this goal? _____

Thoughts
        I will intentionally work on _____
        How will you work on this goal? _____

Body
        I will intentionally work on _____
        How will you work on this goal? _____

I am a STRONG person because_____
I LOVE that I am_____

Today, I will practice self-compassion by: _____
_____
_____
_____

Write a love letter to yourself acknowledging the accomplish-ments you've made thus far.

Dear Self,

Date: /   /   Time   :   am – pm   Location: _____

Today I feel_____ because _____
_____
_____

What are you grateful for today?

I am grateful for _____

I am grateful for _____

I am grateful for _____

                         Daily Goals
Emotional
        I will intentionally work on _____
        How will you work on this goal? _____

Thoughts
        I will intentionally work on _____
        How will you work on this goal? _____

Body
        I will intentionally work on _____
        How will you work on this goal? _____

I am a STRONG person because_____
I LOVE that I am_____

Today, I will practice self-compassion by: _____
_____
_____
_____

Reflections
After completing this Meditation Journal,
What insights have you gained about yourself?

*I am*_____

*I am not*_____

*I have shown progress in*_____

*I am not afraid of*_____

*I have been able to overcome*_____

*I am unique because*_____

*I am consistent in*_____

*I have learned that I*_____

*I love that I am*_____

*I am a strong person because*_____

*I am a good friend because*_____

I will conquer my fear of _____

*I am worthy to be loved because*_____

*I deserve happiness because*_____

I am really surprised that I _____

I have learned to love_____

*I am no longer*_____

*I have gained self-control in*_____

*I will continue to work on*_____

Congratulations! You made it to the end of your meditation journey. You were able to dedicate time and energy to learning more about yourself. Your entries show that you were committed to gaining self-awareness and practicing self-compassion. This meditation journal was created to tailor to your mental, emotional, and physical needs. By simply writing and reflecting through this journal you renewed your thought process and deepened a connection to yourself, the people around you, and to your higher power. My hope is that by incorporating your Body, Soul, and Spirit, you were able to align your true inner self.

Thanks for
mentoring me
and pouring your
love into me
everyday.

Merry Christmas!

Christie Fortenelly MAAT

75033293R00043

Made in the USA
Lexington, KY
17 December 2017